W9-BNO-326

HEROES
OF THE US MILITARY

HEROES OF THE US COAST GUARD

By John M. Shea

Gareth Stevens
Publishing

Please visit our website, www.garethstevens.com. For a free color catalog of all our high-quality books, call toll free 1-800-542-2595 or fax 1-877-542-2596.

Library of Congress Cataloging-in-Publication Data

Shea, John M.
Heroes of the US Coast Guard / John M. Shea.
    pages cm. — (Heroes of the US military)
ISBN 978-1-4339-7241-6 (pbk.)
ISBN 978-1-4339-7242-3 (6-pack)
ISBN 978-1-4339-7240-9 (library binding)
1. United States. Coast Guard—Juvenile literature. I. Title.
VG53.S53 2012
363.28'6092273—dc23

                                    2011052710

First Edition

Published in 2013 by
Gareth Stevens Publishing
111 East 14th Street, Suite 349
New York, NY 10003

Copyright © 2013 Gareth Stevens Publishing

Designer: Michael J. Flynn
Editor: Therese Shea

Photo credits: Cover, p. 1 Rubberball/Frare Davis/Getty Images; courtesy of US Coast Guard: pp. 5 by Chief Mark Coady, 7 by Petty Officer 2nd Class Henry G. Dunphy, 8–9, 10, 11, 13, 14, 18, 21, 23, 25 by Petty Officer 3rd Class Jonathan Lally, 27 by Bobby Nash; p. 6 Universal Images Group/Getty Images; p. 12 courtesy of the Library of Congress; p. 15 courtesy of Popular Science Monthly; pp. 16–17 Three Lions/ Hulton Archive/Getty Images; p. 19 Carl Mydans/Time & Life Pictures/Getty Images; p. 22 Keystone/ Hulton Archive/Getty Images; p. 26 Mario Tama/Getty Images; p. 29 Ilya S. Savenok/Getty Images.

Printed in the United States of America

CPSIA compliance information: Batch #CS12GS: For further information contact Gareth Stevens, New York, New York at 1-800-542-2595.

CONTENTS

Semper Paratus 4

A Call for a Coast Guard 6

The Capture of the *Dart* 8

"The Bravest Woman in America" 10

Breaking Barriers 14

"One of the Bravest Deeds" 16

A Woman of the Resistance 18

Rescue at Guadalcanal 22

Hurricane Katrina 26

Heroic First Day 28

Glossary 30

For More Information 31

Index 32

Words in the glossary appear in **bold** type the first time they are used in the tex

SEMPER PARATUS

The **motto** of the United States Coast Guard is *Semper Paratus*, which is Latin for "always ready." This phrase is fitting for this hardworking branch of the armed forces. It's always watchful and ready to act. Although the Coast Guard is the smallest of the military branches, it's special in that many of its duties focus on peacetime activities.

The Coast Guard has many jobs that reflect its long history. It maintains lighthouses and **buoys** for boat safety. It conducts search-and-rescue operations for missing sailors, fishermen, and swimmers. It also protects the natural world by stopping illegal fishing as well as working to prevent oil and chemical spills.

Four Become One

The US Coast Guard is the combination of four historical services: the US Revenue Cutter Service (or Revenue Marine), the US Lighthouse Service, the US Lifesaving Service, and the Steamboat Inspection Service. When the Revenue Cutter Service was combined with the Lifesaving Service in 1915, it officially became known as the Coast Guard.

Rescuing those in danger is just one of the many responsibilities of the Coast Guard.

5

A CALL FOR A COAST GUARD

After the United States won its independence from England in 1783, it needed revenue. Some of this money came from taxes called tariffs, which were placed on goods brought into the country. However, **smugglers** ignored the tariffs and found ways to bring in goods illegally.

This drawing shows an American military ship battling a pirate ship around 1800.

Alexander Hamilton, the first US Secretary of the Treasury, asked Congress to create an organization to police the waters. The Revenue Marine was formed on August 4, 1790. Because there was no US Navy at this time, the Revenue Marine's **maritime** responsibilities quickly grew. Ships called cutters often defended American vessels from pirates.

Originally a means to increase US revenue, Coast Guard cutters are now symbols of safety and protection along US shores.

Cutters

The Revenue Marine had 10 cutters built that could be used in harbors and on the open sea. Today, the Coast Guard still calls any ship over 65 feet (20 m) long a cutter. A ship smaller than 65 feet is called a boat.

THE CAPTURE OF THE *DART*

During the War of 1812, the British interfered with US trade and even forced American sailors to serve in their navy. The British ship *Dart* alone captured between 20 and 30 American ships in Long Island Sound. In October 1813, the *Dart* stopped in Newport, Rhode Island, where US captain John Cahoone was stationed with his revenue cutter *Vigilant*.

As the *Dart* began to leave Newport Harbor, the *Vigilant* approached rapidly. When the more heavily armed *Dart* was within range, the *Vigilant's* crew fired all the weapons on one side of their ship. Before the British sailors could recover, the *Dart* was boarded and captured by the Americans.

The Royal Navy

During the War of 1812, the British Royal Navy was among the most powerful in the world. It had more than 500 warships, with about 85 in American waters when war broke out. The US Revenue Marine, now called the Revenue Cutter Service, had 16 cutters. The US Navy had just 6 ships.

Because the British had much larger and stronger maritime forces, the victory of the *Vigilant* over the *Dart* represented an important victory for American forces.

"THE BRAVEST WOMAN IN AMERICA"

Idawalley "Ida" Lewis grew up in the Lime Rock Lighthouse in Newport, Rhode Island, where her father was the lighthouse keeper. When he became ill in 1857, 15-year-old Ida helped her mother continue the important duties of the lighthouse.

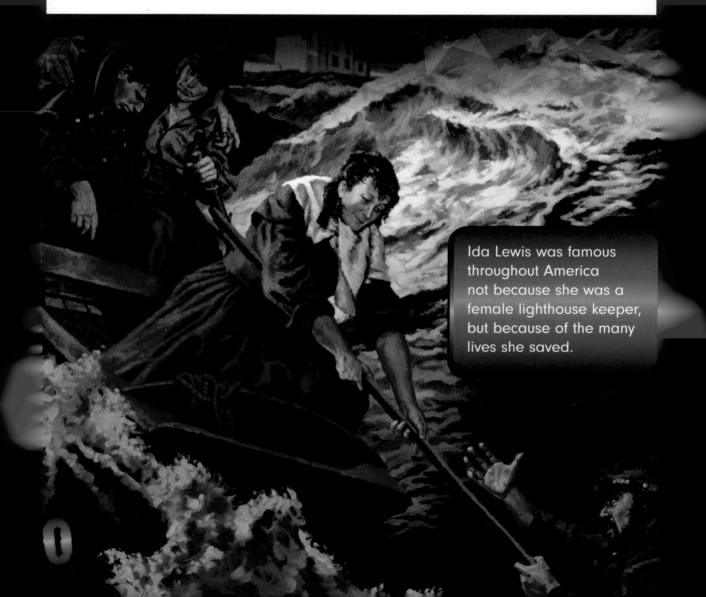

Ida Lewis was famous throughout America not because she was a female lighthouse keeper, but because of the many lives she saved.

At this time, it was unusual for a woman to have a career. However, Lewis's skills and bravery earned her the respect of the US Lighthouse Service and of the nation. She saved her first life at the age of 15! The Lighthouse Service named her the official keeper of Lime Rock Lighthouse in 1879. Lewis would earn her position and fame throughout her life.

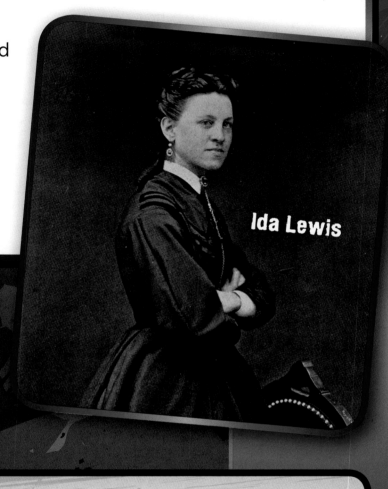

Ida Lewis

Wickies

Lighthouse keepers once lit wicks in oil to make the structure's warning light. If wicks were too short or too long, the flame became dim. The keeper had to keep the wick a perfect length. Because of this, keepers were often referred to as "wickies," even after lighthouses began to use electricity.

Ida Lewis saved at least 18 people over her 39 years of service. She received a gold medal from the US Lifesaving Service in 1881 for rescuing two soldiers who had fallen through ice. Risking her own life, she crossed the ice with a rope and managed to pull both men to safety.

Many stories were published about Ida. She appeared on the cover of *Harper's Weekly*, a popular magazine of the time. President Ulysses Grant even made a special trip to meet her. She was named "The Bravest Woman in America" by the Society of the American Cross of Honor.

Ida Lewis died in 1911, while she was on duty in her lighthouse.

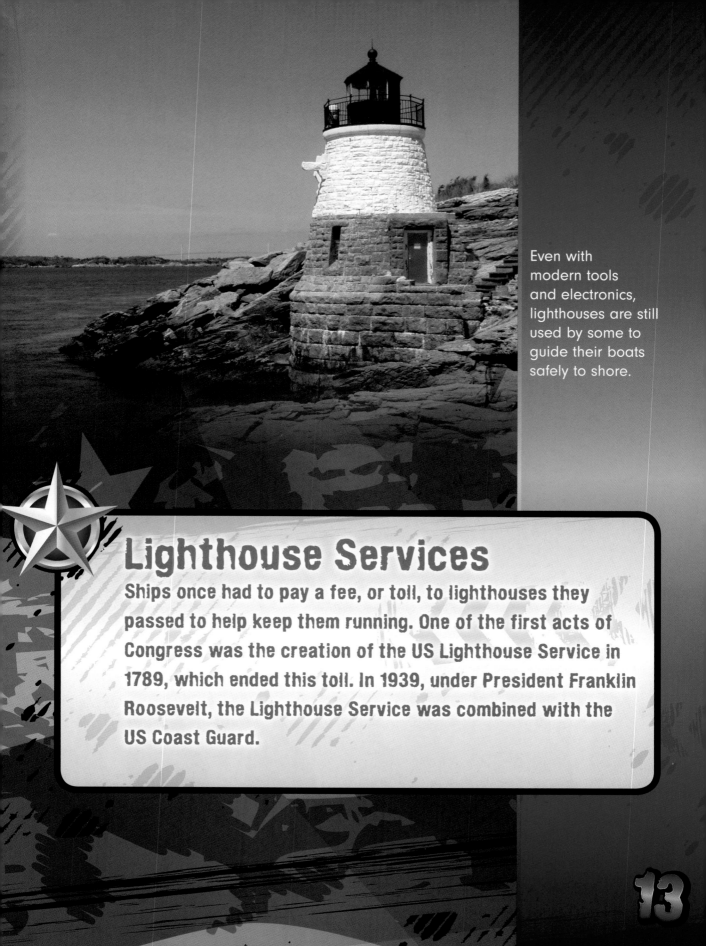

Even with modern tools and electronics, lighthouses are still used by some to guide their boats safely to shore.

Lighthouse Services

Ships once had to pay a fee, or toll, to lighthouses they passed to help keep them running. One of the first acts of Congress was the creation of the US Lighthouse Service in 1789, which ended this toll. In 1939, under President Franklin Roosevelt, the Lighthouse Service was combined with the US Coast Guard.

BREAKING BARRIERS

In 1880, Richard Etheridge, an African American, was given command of the Pea Island Lifesaving Station near North Carolina. Etheridge was the first black lighthouse keeper in the Lifesaving Service.

Richard Etheridge is shown here with his crew in front of the station. The photo was taken around 1890.

In October 1896, the ship *E. S. Newman* was wrecked offshore by a violent storm. Etheridge and his men were unable to reach the crew by boat, and it was too windy to use a Lyle gun to shoot a rope into the water. Etheridge commanded his men to tie ropes to each other and swim out to the ship. After a total of 10 trips, they rescued all the ship's passengers.

The Lyle Gun

Getting rope from shore to a sinking ship was risky to both rescuers and those in trouble. In 1878, David Lyle invented a cannon-like gun that could shoot a line more than 600 yards (549 m) from the shore. The gun could also be used to help people who had fallen through ice.

"ONE OF THE BRAVEST DEEDS"

On August 16, 1918, a German **U-boat** attacked the British oil tanker *Mirlo* off the Outer Banks of North Carolina. The tanker exploded and covered the water with oil, which then caught on fire.

John Allen Midgett, Coast Guard commander of the Chicamacomico Lifeboat Station, heard the powerful explosion and got his crew ready for action. Battling rough waves and leaping flames for almost 7 hours, Midgett and his team rescued all but 10 of the *Mirlo's* crew. The captain of the *Mirlo* said the rescue was "one of the bravest deeds" he had ever seen. Midgett and his men were honored by both the British and American governments.

U-boats

Although submarines had limited uses in other wars, World War I was the first in which submarines played an important role. U-boats didn't only pose a danger to American ships in open waters, they also provided a **stealth** means of bringing enemies onto American soil.

German U-boats, like the one pictured on the right, played an important role in World War I. In fact, the sinking of the *Lusitania* by a U-boat in 1915 caused many Americans to want to join the war against Germany.

A WOMAN OF THE RESISTANCE

Florence Ebersole Smith Finch was born in the Philippines to a Filipino mother and a retired US Army father. She worked for US Intelligence in Manila. There, she met and married Charles Smith of the US Navy.

On January 2, 1942, Japanese forces attacked and occupied Manila. Though Americans on the island were captured, Finch was able to hide her connection to the United States. She was put to work at a fuel factory. A month later, she learned that her husband had been killed in action. Finch turned her grief into determination to help the **resistance** battle the Japanese.

Florence Ebersole Smith Finch

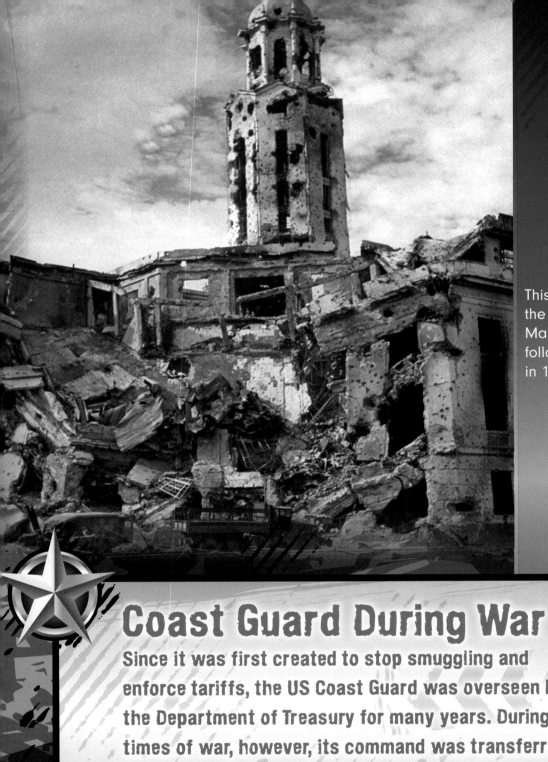

This photo shows the ruins of Manila's city hall following a battle in 1945.

Coast Guard During War

Since it was first created to stop smuggling and enforce tariffs, the US Coast Guard was overseen by the Department of Treasury for many years. During times of war, however, its command was transferred to the US Navy. Since 2003, the Department of Homeland Security has overseen the Coast Guard.

Florence Finch gave supplies to those fighting against the Japanese. She also snuck food and medicine to prisoners of war. She assisted in acts of **sabotage** against the Japanese military as well. However, Japanese forces finally discovered her actions. In October 1944, she was captured, imprisoned, and tortured.

Finch was freed by US forces in February 1945 and traveled to her father's family in New York. She soon joined the Coast Guard and continued to serve the United States. Because of her brave actions, she received the Medal of Freedom. She was also the first woman to receive the Asiatic-Pacific Campaign Ribbon.

Medal of Freedom

President Harry Truman created the Medal of Freedom in 1945 to recognize and celebrate civilians who had helped the United States in the war effort. In 1963, John F. Kennedy renamed the award the Presidential Medal of Freedom and included those who contributed to world peace as well as to the nation's cultural history.

Despite her incredible bravery, Florence Finch said, "I feel very humble because my activities in the war effort were **trivial** compared with those of people who gave their lives for their country."

21

RESCUE AT GUADALCANAL

During World War II, American and Japanese forces fought one another for control of many islands in the Pacific Ocean. The island of Guadalcanal, which lies northeast of Australia, was important to both sides because of its location. In the summer of 1942, American forces attempted to recapture the island from Japanese control.

This photo shows American marines coming ashore at Guadalcanal in August 1942.

Coastguardsman Douglas A. Munro was in charge of the ships that transported US marines to the island. After successfully completing his mission, Munro returned to his base. He soon learned that the marines were badly outnumbered and not likely to survive. Munro immediately offered to command a rescue **mission**.

Douglas A. Munro

Roles in World War II

During World War II, the Coast Guard was important in transporting soldiers around the globe. They delivered troops and ships to the beaches of Normandy, France, and sailed marines to the Pacific Islands. More than 240,000 men and women served in the Coast Guard during World War II. Of those, 574 were killed in action.

Munro led the boats back to the trapped marines. As the American soldiers boarded the rescue ships, weapon fire from the Japanese increased, making it harder for the remaining marines to reach the boats.

Munro steered his ship so that it provided cover for the escaping marines. He drew the enemy's fire away from the marines but toward himself. As the last US marines boarded, Munro was fatally wounded. His last words were "Did they get off?" He died knowing that he had saved many lives. For his selfless bravery, Douglas A. Munro received the Medal of Honor.

Medal of Honor

The Medal of Honor is the highest award the United States gives to members of the armed forces. Begun by Congress in 1861, it was originally created to recognize heroes during the American Civil War. As of 2011, a total of 3,458 people had received this award.

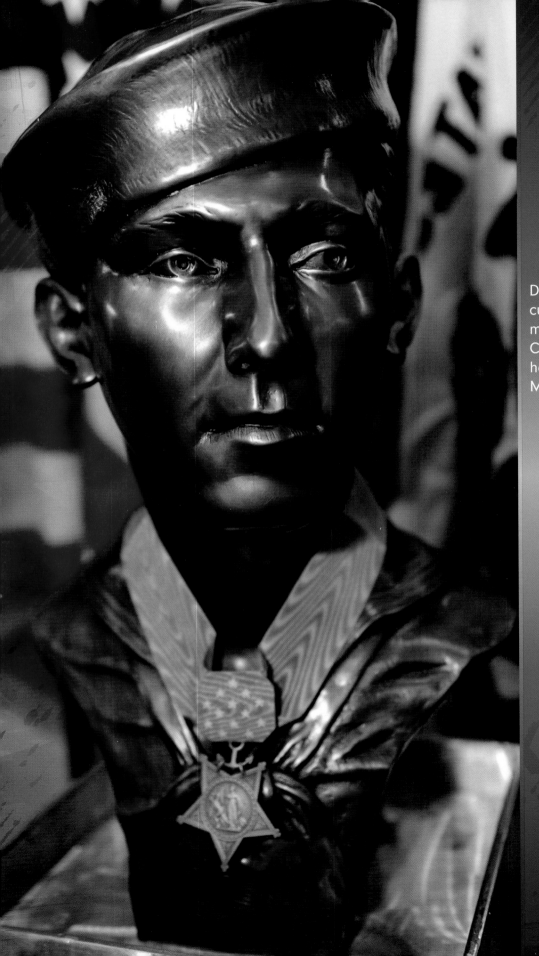

Douglas Munro is currently the only member of the Coast Guard to have received the Medal of Honor.

HURRICANE KATRINA

In August 2005, Hurricane Katrina caused one of the worst national **disasters** in American history. New Orleans, Louisiana, was especially hit hard. The storm left 80 percent of the city under 20 feet (6 m) of water. About 60,000 people were trapped in their homes. Many climbed onto their rooftops for safety.

Living up to their motto of being always ready, the US Coast Guard responded to one of America's largest national disasters by rescuing thousands of people.

U.S. COAST GUARD   181228

A coastguardsman looks on as about 1,000 New Orleans residents fleeing Hurricane Katrina arrive in a safe harbor.

The Coast Guard responded to the disaster with the largest search-and-rescue operation in American history. It involved about 5,600 service members. The Coast Guard rescued more than 33,500 people from New Orleans. They also organized the removal of more than 9,000 medical patients and took them to safer hospitals.

All in a Day's Work

Even in times of peace and without natural disasters, the Coast Guard is hard at work. Every day, the US Coast Guard conducts an average of 64 search-and-rescue operations. They save about 12 lives each day.

HEROIC FIRST DAY

Christopher Austin's first day as a Coast Guard rescue swimmer was December 18, 2010. That same day, rough waves near Willapa Bay, Washington, overturned a fishing boat, throwing two men into the icy waters.

Austin's rescue helicopter located one of the victims, and Austin was lowered into the water to recover him. The cold, choppy seas made the rescue hard, but Austin got the man into the helicopter and performed **CPR** on the way to the hospital. Austin earned the honor of becoming the United Service Organizations (USO) Coast Guardsman of the Year. His actions remind us that even the newest member of the Coast Guard is "always ready" to save a life.

Rescue Swimmers

Rescue swimmers are among the most highly trained members of the Coast Guard. They have incredible strength and must be able to swim in cold and dangerous waters for at least 30 minutes. They also learn advanced first aid. The training is so demanding that more than half of those who begin don't finish.

Thanks to Austin's efforts, the rescued fisherman made a complete recovery.

GLOSSARY

buoy: a floating object used to guide ships

CPR: stands for "cardiopulmonary resuscitation." It is used to try to restart breathing and heartbeat in someone whose heart has stopped.

disaster: an event that causes much suffering or loss

maritime: having to do with the sea

mission: a task or job a group must perform

motto: a short saying that expresses a rule to live by

resistance: in wartime, a group of people who take secret action against the enemy

revenue: the income of a government

sabotage: to cause damage in order to weaken an enemy's power

smuggler: one who takes goods into or out of a country illegally

stealth: done quietly, so as not to be noticed

trivial: unimportant

U-boat: a German submarine (short for *Unterseeboot*, or "undersea boat")

FOR MORE INFORMATION

Books

David, Jack. *United States Coast Guard*. Minneapolis, MN: Bellwether Media, 2008.

Noble, Dennis. *The U.S. Coast Guard*. Milwaukee, WI: World Almanac Library, 2005.

Websites

Congressional Medal of Honor Society
www.cmohs.org
The Congressional Medal of Honor website tells the history of the medal as well as the biographies of the brave people who have earned it.

United States Coast Guard
www.uscg.mil
This official website for the United States Coast Guard has a wealth of information on the organization.

United States Coast Guard Academy
www.cga.edu
The Coast Guard Academy website describes in detail what it takes to serve in America's oldest maritime armed force.

INDEX

Asiatic-Pacific Campaign Ribbon 20

Austin, Christopher 28, 29

"Bravest Woman in America, The" 12

Cahoone, John 8

Chicamacomico Lifeboat Station 17

Dart 8, 9

Department of Homeland Security 19

Department of the Treasury 19

E. S. Newman 15

Etheridge, Richard 14, 15

Finch, Florence Ebersole Smith 18, 20, 21

Guadalcanal 22

Hurricane Katrina 26, 27

Lewis, Idawalley "Ida" 10, 11, 12

lighthouse keeper 10, 11, 14

lighthouses 4, 10, 11, 12, 13

Lime Rock Lighthouse 10, 11

Lyle, David 15

Lyle gun 15

Medal of Freedom 20

Medal of Honor 24, 25

Midgett, John Allen 17

Mirlo 16, 17

Munro, Douglas A. 23, 24, 25

Pea Island Lifesaving Station 14

pirates 6, 7

rescue swimmer 28

search-and-rescue operations 4, 27

smugglers 6, 19

Steamboat Inspection Service 4

tariffs 6, 19

United Service Organizations Coast Guardsman of the Year 28

US Lifesaving Service 4, 12, 14

US Lighthouse Service 4, 11, 13

US Revenue Cutter Service (Revenue Marine) 4, 7, 9

Vigilant 8, 9

War of 1812 8, 9

World War I 17

World War II 22, 23